THE
NOVENA

THE STORY OF
OUR LADY OF PERPETUAL HELP

An 'icon' is a Christian picture which tells a story or teaches a truth. Traditionally, icons have been associated with the Eastern Church, but have played a part in the Western Church also. The icon of our Lady of Perpetual Help (or 'Perpetual Succour') is an icon which tells of the Passion and death of Jesus, and of the suffering of Mary his mother.

The original picture of Our Lady of Perpetual Help was painted on the island of Crete over five-hundred years ago. The picture was stolen by a merchant in 1498 and brought by him from Crete to Rome the following year. It is recorded in the history of the picture that the merchant fell seriously ill, and fearing death he asked a friend to place the picture in a church where it could once again be seen by the faithful. The merchant died, but his friend held onto the picture and it was placed by his wife in their house. After a series of visions of Our Lady, the friend was finally convinced to part with the picture and place it, in accordance with Our Lady's request, in the Church of St Matthew in Rome. The Church of St Matthew was destroyed in 1798, but the picture was kept safe by the Augustinian friars. Only when a new church was eventually built on the site of the old St Matthew's could Our Lady's request be fulfilled once again. The new church was the Redemptorist church of St Alphonsus, the obvious place for the picture, so near to its former home. And so the Pope requested that the picture be moved to the Redemptorist church.

On April 26th 1866 the picture of Our Lady of Perpetual Help was solemnly installed in this new church of St Alphonsus in Rome. The first copy of the picture to leave Rome came to Bishop Eton, the Redemptorist church in Liverpool, England. Since then, copies of the picture have been taken to the four corners of the world. Devotion to Our Lady of Perpetual Help, through Novenas and private prayers, continues to spread. 'Our Lady of Perpetual Help' is one of the best known and best loved icons in the world.

Greek initials for Archangel Michael, who holds the lance and the sponge. 'Michael' means 'who is like God?'

Greek initials for Archangel Gabriel, who holds the cross of Christ. 'Gabriel' means 'God is strong.'

Mary's mouth is small, symbolising her few recorded words and the depth of her contemplation.

Greek initials for Jesus Christ.

Greek initials for Mother of God.

Gold background symbolises heaven.

Red tunic, the colour worn by virgins at the time of Christ.

The Christ-child clings trustingly to his mother.

The mother's supporting hand.

The colour blue, worn by mothers in Palestine.

The falling sandal indicating his alarm at the thought of his Passion and death.

3

THE NOVENA
NINE DAYS OF PRAYER

After the resurrection Jesus appeared to his disciples. He told them to wait in Jerusalem for the descent of the Holy Spirit. A Novena echoes this prayer of waiting and is a traditional way of coming together to pray. Together with Our Lady of Perpetual Help, we too pray to God, in thanksgiving, in petition and in praise.

The Novena is either spread over nine days or is prayed weekly (the 'Perpetual Novena'). The Novena is usually prayed together in church, but may be prayed at home.

This Novena is based on the song of Our Lady at the Visitation, the hymn called the Magnificat (Luke 1:46-55). We ask Our Lady, under the title Our Lady of Perpetual Help, to pray with us and for us. It is good to pray; it is important to pray; we read in the Acts of the Apostles that '....with one heart all the apostles joined constantly in prayer, together with some women, including Mary the mother of Jesus....'

Contents

OUTLINE OF SERVICE

1. HYMN

2. OPENING PRAYER

3. PSALM

4. SCRIPTURE READING

5. SERMON

6. THANKSGIVING

7. NOVENA PRAYER

8. PETITIONS/LITANY

9. MAGNIFICAT/EXPOSITION OF THE BLESSED SACRAMENT

10. CONCLUDING PRAYER & BLESSING

11. HYMN

The hymns, psalms and prayers in the Novena service may be varied: a selection of alternatives is provided.

The readings from Morning and Evening Prayer of the Church are especially suitable for use in the Novena. Where appropriate, these can be of the liturgical season — Advent, Lent, etc.

The sermon may be based on the reading or on some aspect of faith. Alternatively, a short time of silence may be observed.

During the Novena Prayer, petitions may be read out. Otherwise a litany may be said. During the Magnificat the Blessed Sacrament may be exposed, followed by a time of silent prayer.

A selection of concluding prayers is included.

The Novena may be led by a priest, deacon or another person.

NOVENA SERVICE

HYMN

Holy Virgin, by God's decree,
you were called eternally;
that he could give his Son to our race.
Mary, we praise you, hail, full of grace.

R. Ave, ave, ave, Maria

By your faith and loving accord,
as the handmaid of the Lord,
you undertook God's plan to embrace.
Mary we thank you, hail, full of grace. **(R.)**

Joy to God you gave and expressed,
of all women none more blessed,
when in mankind your Son took his place.
Mary, we love you, hail, full of grace. **(R.)**

Refuge for your children so weak,
sure protection all can seek.
Problems of life you help us to face.
Mary, we trust you, hail, full of grace. **(R.)**

To our needy world of today
love and beauty you portray,
showing the path to Christ we must trace.
Mary, our mother, hail, full of grace. **(R.)**

OPENING PRAYER

(When praying the Novena at home, say all the prayers yourself)

Leader: Sisters and brothers, we have come before the picture of our Mother of Perpetual Help, that she will pray with us to God, in praise, in petition, and in thanksgiving.

All: Dear Mother of Perpetual Help, throughout your life you were open to God's Holy Spirit: faithful in prayer, willing in obedience and generous in love. Pray for us, that we may be open to God's word and filled with the Holy Spirit. You were faithful in prayer; pray that we too may follow Christ your son with the same spirit of prayer, with a willing heart, and in love for him, who first loved us.

PSALM *(alternative psalms pages 17—22)*

Psalm (115) God has done so much for us — what can we do in return?

> **All:** I trusted, even when I said:
> "I am sorely afflicted",
> and when I said in my alarm:
> "There is no one I can trust".
>
> How can I repay the Lord
> for his goodness to me?
> The cup of salvation I will raise;
> I will call on the Lord's name.
>
> My vows to the Lord I will fulfill
> before all his people.
> O precious in the eyes of the Lord
> is the death of his faithful.
>
> Your servant, Lord, your servant am I;
> you have loosened my bonds.
> A thanksgiving sacrifice I make;
> I will call on the Lord's name.
>
> My vows to the Lord I will fulfill
> before all his people,
> in the courts of the house of the Lord,
> in your midst, O Jerusalem.

SCRIPTURE READING

SHORT SERMON
(or a time of silence to reflect on the word of God)

THANKSGIVING

Leader: Let us pause for a moment and call to mind what God has done for us. (pause) And let us now give thanks for the goodness of creation, and for all the graces we have received.

For the beauty of all that you have made

> **R. Lord, we thank you.**

For your loving mercy. **(R)**

For our salvation. **(R)**

For the consolation of the Holy Spirit. **(R)**

For the promise of your glory. **(R)**

For our family and friends. **(R)**

For faith. **(R)**

For Mary, our Mother of Perpetual Help. **(R)**

NOVENA PRAYER

Leader: Let us now turn to Our Lady asking her to pray for us.

All: Dear Mother,
The Lord looked on you in your humility, and chose you to be the mother of his son; and now all ages call you blessed. God has worked marvels for you. You witnessed the death of your son on the cross, and your continuing faith brought you to witness his victory over death, filling your heart with joy and praise. By the example of your life, you showed that God's mercy is on those who fear him. You sang of the justice of the one who casts the mighty from their thrones and raises the lowly; you told of the promise made to Abraham, Sarah, and all their descendants for ever. You are now with the saints, singing the praises of God, and praying for us, who need your prayers. Pray with us to the Lord, and as our prayers arise before him like incense, he will hear us and answer us, according to his promise.

PETITIONS and **GENERAL INTENTIONS** are mentioned here or a Litany may be said.

When we feel burdened by sickness or old age,

> **R.** Holy Mary, Mother of God, Pray for us.

That we may forgive those who hurt us, **(R.)**
That we might have peace of mind, **(R.)**
That families might increase in love and respect for each other and for God, (R.)
That single people may be blessed by God, **(R.)**
That those preparing for marriage may always grow in love, **(R.)**
That the hurt caused by broken relationships might be healed, **(R.)**
That those who mourn be comforted, **(R.)**
That those who seek work will find it, **(R.)**
That the homeless will find shelter, **(R.)**
That the hungry will be fed, **(R.)**
That unjust discrimination will cease, **(R.)**
That those called to Religious life and priesthood may be faithful to their call, (R.)
That all who have lost their faith will find it again, **(R.)**
That all Christians may be united in faith and love, **(R.)**

Leader: Let us pray.

All: Almighty God, our creator, see us your children gathered in prayer, with Mary the mother of your Son. As we ask, let us receive; as we search, may we find; and as we knock, may the door be opened. And may your will be done, on earth as it is in heaven. **Amen.**

MAGNIFICAT

My Soul proclaims you, mighty God,
My spirit sings your praise!
You look on me, you lift me up,
and gladness fills my days.

All nations now will share my joy,
Your gifts you have outpoured;
Your little one you have made great;
I magnify my God!

For those who love your holy name,
Your mercy will not die.
Your strong right arm puts down the proud,
And lifts the lowly high.

You fill the hungry with good things,
The rich you send away.
The promise made to Abraham
Is filled to endless day.

Magnificat, Magnificat,
Magnificat, Praise God;
Praise God, praise God,
praise God, praise God,
Magnificat, Praise God!   *tune: Amazing Grace*

*(During the Magnificat the Blessed Sacrament may be exposed.
There may be a time of silent prayer; the Blessing may be given;
a Eucharistic hymn may be sung.*

*When the Blessed Sacrament is not exposed, or when the
Novena is prayed at home, a few moments of silent prayer in
praise of God may follow the Magnificat.)*

CONCLUDING PRAYER & BLESSING

Leader: God our Father, help us to be faithful witnesses to your mercy and love. May we bring to others the gifts we receive from you. Give us grateful hearts that we may thank you, stronger faith that we may trust you, and a vision of your glory that we may praise you.

And may Almighty God bless you, in the name of the Father, and of the Son, and of the Holy Spirit. Amen.

or *(when the leader is not a priest or deacon, or the Novena is prayed at home):*

May the Lord bless us, keep us from evil, and bring us to everlasting life. Amen.

HYMN

1. As I kneel before you,
   As I bow my head in prayer,
   take this day, make it yours
   and fill me with your love.

   > **R.** Ave Maria, gratia plena,
   >   Dominus tecum, benedicta tu.

2. All I have I give you,
   ev'ry dream and wish are yours.
   Mother of Christ, Mother of mine,
   present them to my Lord. **(R.)**

3. As I kneel before you,
   and I see your smiling face,
   ev'ry thought, ev'ry word
   is lost in your embrace. **(R.)**

HYMNS, PSALMS AND PRAYERS

1
1. Mary, from thy sacred image
With those eyes so sadly sweet,
Mother of Perpetual Succour!
See us kneeling at thy feet.

2. In thy arms thy child thou bearest,
Source of all thy joy and woe;
What thy bliss, how deep thy sorrows
Mother, thou alone canst know.

2
Salve Regina, Mater misericordiae,
vita, dulcedo, et spes nostra, salve.
Ad te clamamus, exules filii Hevae.
Ad te suspiramus, gementes et flentes,
in hac lacrimarum vale.
Eia ergo, advocata nostra,
illos tuos misericordes oculos
ad nos converte.
Et Jesum benedictum fructum ventris tui,
nobis post hoc exilium ostende.
O clemens, O pia, O dulcis Virgo Maria.

3
1. O Mother blest, whom God bestows
   on sinners and on just,
   what joy, what hope thou givest those
   who in thy mercy trust.

   R. *Thou art clement, thou art chaste,*
      Mary, thou art fair;
      of all mothers sweetest, best;
      none with thee compare.

2. O heavenly mother, mistress sweet!
   It never yet was told
   that suppliant sinner left thy feet
   unpitied, unconsoled. (R.)

3. O mother pitiful and mild,
   cease not to pray for me;
   for I do love thee as a child,
   and sigh for love of thee. (R.)

4. Most powerful mother, all men know
   thy son denies thee nought;
   thou askest, wishest it, and lo!
   his power thy will hath wrought. (R.)

5. O mother blest, for me obtain
   ungrateful though I be,
   to love that God who first could deign
   to show such love for me. (R.)

St Alphonsus Liguori

4 I sing the Lord God's praises,
   I answer to his call.
   His servant-girl he raises,
   she will be blessed by all.
   The Lord God gives his power
   to her who loves his name;
   o'er her his strength will tower,
   his mercies will remain.

   Proud-hearted men he scatters,
   the strong will pass away;
   and for the kind and gentle
   there dawns the Lord's own day.
   Woe to the rich and mighty!
   He feeds and satisfies
   those who for justice hunger,
   and to him turn their eyes.

   A Saviour he had promised
   to Abram long ago;
   and now to his own people
   his mercy he will show.
   Come let us praise our Father,
   for he fulfils his word,
   and sends his Holy Spirit
   through Jesus Christ our Lord

W.F. Harwood

5

1. Mary, let Perpetual Succour
   Be the answer to our prayer;
   For thy son, of all the wretched
   Gives to thee perpetual care.
   Ever ready help hast thou,
   Let thy children feel it now.

2. Though we try to rise, yet ever
   Down in misery we fall;
   So like feeble children sadly,
   For our mother's help we call.
   Ever ready help hast thou.
   Let thy children feel it now.

6

Sing of Mary, pure and lowly,
virgin mother undefiled.
Sing of God's own Son most holy,
who became her little child.
Fairest child of fairest mother,
God the Lord, who came to earth,
Word made flesh, our very brother,
takes our nature by his birth.

Sing of Jesus, son of Mary,
in the home at Nazareth.
Toil and labour cannot weary
love enduring unto death.
Constant was the love he gave her,
though he went forth from her side,
forth to preach and heal and suffer,
till on Calvary he died.

Glory be to God the Father,
glory be to God the Son,
glory be to God the Spirit,
glory to the three in one.
From the heart of blessed Mary,
from all saints the song ascends,
and the Church the strain re-echoes
unto earth's remotest ends.

Anonymous

7 1. O bread of heaven, beneath this veil
thou dost my very God conceal;
my Jesus, dearest treasure, hail;
I love thee and adoring kneel;
each loving soul by thee is fed
with thine own self in form of bread.

2. O food of life, thou who dost give
the pledge of immortality;
I live; no, 'tis not I that live;
God gives me life, God lives in me:
he feeds my soul, he guides my ways,
and every grief with joy repays.

3. O bond of love, that dost unite
the servant to his living Lord;
could I dare live, and not requite
such love then death were meet reward:
I cannot live unless to prove
some love for such unmeasured love.

4. Beloved Lord in heaven above,
where, Jesus, thou awaitest me;
to gaze on thee with changeless love,
yes, thus I hope, thus shall it be:
for how can he deny me heaven
who here on earth himself hath given?
St Alphonsus Liguori

8 1. O saving victim, opening wide
The gate of heav'n to man below;
Our foes press on from ev'ry side;
Thine aid supply, thy strength bestow.

2. To thy great name be endless praise,
Immortal Godhead, one in three;
O grant us endless length of days
In our true native land with thee. Amen.

9 1. Therefore we, before him bending,
This great sacrament revere;
Types and shadows have their ending,
For the newer rite is here;
Faith, our outward sense befriending,
Makes the inward vision clear.

2. Glory let us give, and blessing
To the Father and the Son,
Honour, might, and praise addressing,
While eternal ages run;
Ever too his love confessing
Who from both, with both is one. Amen.

PSALMS

Psalm 46

Even in the midst of adversity, God is with us. With God on our side, who could stand against us?

> God is for us a refuge and strength,
> a helper close at hand, in time of distress,
> so we shall not fear though the earth should rock,
> though the mountains fall into the depths of the sea;
> even though its waters rage and foam,
> even though the mountains be shaken by its waves.
>
> The Lord of hosts is with us;
> the God of Jacob is our stronghold.
>
> The waters of a river give joy to God's city,
> the holy place where the Most High dwells.
> God is within, it cannot be shaken;
> God will help it at the dawning of the day.
> Nations are in tumult, kingdoms are shaken;
> he lifts his voice, the earth shrinks away.
>
> The Lord of hosts is with us;
> the God of Jacob is our stronghold.
>
> Come, consider the works of the Lord,
> the redoubtable deeds he has done on the earth.
> He puts an end to wars over all the earth;
> the bow he breaks, the spear he snaps.
> He burns the shields with fire.
> "Be still and know that I am God,
> supreme among the nations, supreme on the earth!"
>
> The Lord of hosts is with us;
> the God of Jacob is our stronghold.

Psalm 24

God created the heavens and the earth. Those who seek God will share in his life.

The Lord's is the earth and its fullness,
the world and all its peoples.
It is he who set it on the seas;
on the waters he made it firm.

Who shall climb the mountain of the Lord?
Who shall stand in his holy place?
Those with clean hands and pure heart,
who desire not worthless things,
who have not sworn so as to deceive their neighbour.

They shall receive blessings from the Lord
and reward from the God who saves them.
These are the ones who seek him,
seek the face of the God of Jacob.

O gates, lift high your heads;
grow higher, ancient doors.
Let him enter, the king of glory!

Who is the king of glory?
The Lord, the mighty, the valiant,
the Lord, the valiant in war.

O gates, lift high your heads;
grow higher, ancient doors.
Let him enter, the king of glory!

Who is he, the king of glory?
He, the Lord of armies,
he is the king of glory.

Psalm 113

God is great and deserves our praise.

Alleluia!

Praise, O servants of the Lord,
praise the name of the Lord!
May the name of the Lord be blessed
both now and for evermore!
From the rising of the sun to its setting
praised be the name of the Lord!

High above all nations is the Lord,
above the heavens his glory.
Who is like the Lord, our God,
who has risen on high to his throne
yet stoops from the heights to look down,
to look down upon heaven and earth?

From the dust he lifts up the lowly,
from the dungheap he raises the poor
to set them in the company of rulers,
yes, with the rulers of his people.
To the childless wife he gives a home
and gladdens her heart with children.

Psalm 116

To be a Christian is to admit that we need God's help. In God is
our life.

Alleluia!

I love the Lord for he has heard
the cry of my appeal;
for he turned his ear to me
in the day when I called him.

They surrounded me, the snares of death,
with the anguish of the tomb;
they caught me, sorrow and distress.
I called on the Lord's name.

O Lord my God, deliver me!

How gracious is the Lord and just;
our God has compassion.
The Lord protects the simple hearts;
I was helpless so he saved me.

Turn back, my soul, to your rest
for the Lord has been good;
he has kept my soul from death,
my eyes from tears,
my feet from stumbling.

I will walk in the presence of the Lord
in the land of the living.

Psalm 130

Our God hears our prayers, forgives us and saves us.

Out of the depths I cry to you, O Lord,
Lord, hear my voice!
O let your ears be attentive
to the voice of my pleading.

If you, O Lord, should mark our guilt,
Lord, who would survive?
But with you is found forgiveness:
for this we revere you.

My soul is waiting for the Lord.
I count on his word.
My soul is longing for the Lord
more than those who watch for daybreak.
Let the watchers count on daybreak
and Israel on the Lord.

Because with the Lord there is mercy
and fulness of redemption,
Israel indeed he will redeem
from all its iniquity.

Psalm 42 — Part 1

There is a longing in us that only God can satisfy. We know that when we are in God we are at home.

> Like the deer that yearns
> for running streams,
> so my soul is yearning
> for you, my God.
>
> My soul is thirsting for God,
> the God of my life;
> when can I enter and see
> the face of God?
>
> My tears have become my bread,
> by night, by day,
> as I hear it said all the day long:
> "Where is your God?"
>
> These things will I remember
> as I pour out my soul:
> how I would lead the rejoicing crowd
> into the house of God,
> amid cries of gladness and thanksgiving,
> the throng wild with joy.
>
> Why are you cast down, my soul,
> why groan within me?
> Hope in God; I will praise him still,
> my saviour and my God.

My soul is cast down within me
as I think of you,
from the country of Jordan and Mount Hermon,
from the Hill of Mizar.

Deep is calling on deep,
in the roar of waters;
your torrents and all your waves
swept over me.

By day the Lord will send
his loving kindness;
by night I will sing to him,
praise the God of my life.

I will say to God, my rock:
"Why have you forgotten me?
Why do I go mourning
oppressed by the foe?"

With cries that pierce me to the heart,
my enemies revile me,
saying to me all the day long:
"Where is your God?"

Why are you cast down, my soul,
why groan within me?
Hope in God; I will praise him still,
my saviour and my God.

LITANIES

1 That we may be faithful to prayer,

> **R. Pray with us, O Mother.**

That we may have courage in all our trials, **(R.)**
That we may always call on the mercy of God, **(R.)**
That we may faithfully follow God's will in our lives, **(R.)**
In time of sickness in the home, **(R.)**
When we are in need, **(R.)**
In misunderstandings with those we love, **(R.)**
For peace in our homes, **(R.)**
That those who govern our country may act wisely, justly
and for the good of all, **(R.)**
That we may see our daily lives as service to our neighbour, **(R.)**
That we may be tolerant and patient with others, **(R.)**
For the church, the body of Christ, **(R.)**
For peace in our world, **(R.)**
That all people will come to know Christ, **(R.)**

2 You listened to the Lord:

> **R. Pray for us.**

You were obedient to God's will. **(R.)**
You were overshadowed by the Spirit. **(R.)**
You conceived God's son. **(R.)**
You shared your joy with Elizabeth. **(R.)**
You were loved and cherished by Joseph **(R.)**
You gave birth to Jesus in Bethlehem. **(R.)**
You raised the child Jesus. **(R.)**
You pondered the Word of God. **(R.)**
You believed in your son. **(R.)**
You saw Jesus suffer. **(R.)**
You stood by the cross. **(R.)**
You saw your son die. **(R.)**
You visited his tomb. **(R.)**
You witnessed his glorious new life. **(R.)**
You rejoiced in his ascension into heaven. **(R.)**
You prayed for the coming of the Spirit. **(R.)**
You received the Holy Spirit at Pentecost. **(R.)**
You were there at the birth of the Church. **(R.)**
You completed the task God created you to do. **(R.)**
You were raised up to the glory of heaven. **(R.)**

MAGNIFICAT

1 My soul glorifies the Lord,
my spirit rejoices in God , my saviour.
He looks on his servant in her lowliness;
henceforth all ages will call me blessed.

The Almighty works marvels for me.
Holy his name!
His mercy is from age to age,
on those who fear him.

He puts forth his arm in strength
and scatters the proud-hearted.
He casts the mighty from their thrones
and raises the lowly.

He fills the starving with good things,
sends the rich away empty.

He protects Israel , his servant,
remembering his mercy,
the mercy promised to our fathers,
to Abraham and his sons for ever.

2 God fills me with joy, Alleluia
His holy presence is my robe, Alleluia.

My soul now glorify
The Lord who is my saviour.
Rejoice for who am I,
That God has shown me favour.

The world shall call me blessed,
and ponder on my story.
In me is manifest,
God's greatness and his glory.

For those who are his friends
and keep his laws as holy
his mercy never ends,
and he exalts the lowly.

But by his pow'r the great,
the proud, the self conceited,
The kings who sit in state,
Are humbled and defeated.

He feeds the starving poor,
He guards his holy nation,
Fulfilling what he swore
Long since in revelation.

Then glorify with me,
The Lord who is my saviour;
One holy Trinity,
For ever and for ever.

3 Tell out, my soul, the greatness of the Lord!
unnumbered blessings, give my spirit voice;
tender to me the promise of his Word;
in God my Saviour shall my heart rejoice.

Tell out, my soul, the greatness of his name!
Make known his might, the deeds his arm has done;
his mercy sure, from age to age the same;
his holy name — the Lord, the Mighty One.

Tell out, my soul, the greatness of his might!
Powers and dominions lay their glory by.
Proud hearts and stubborn wills are put to flight,
the hungry fed, the humble lifted high.

Tell out, my soul, the glories of his Word!
Firm is his promise, and his mercy sure.
Tell out my soul, the greatness of the Lord;
to children's children and for evermore!

Timothy Dudley-Smith

4 My soul is filled with joy
as I sing to God my saviour:
he has looked upon his servant
he has visited his people.

And holy is his name
through all generations!
Everlasting is his mercy
to the people he has chosen,
and holy is his name!

I am lowly as a child,
but I know from this day forward
that my name will be remembered,
for all will call me blessed.

I proclaim the pow'r of God!
He does marvels for his servants;
though he scatters the proud hearted
and destroys the might of princes.

To the hungry he gives food,
sends the rich away empty.
In his mercy he is mindful
of the people he has chosen.

In his love he now fulfills
what he promised to our fathers.
I will praise the Lord, my saviour.
Everlasting is his mercy.

SEASONAL PRAYERS

ADVENT: Creator God, you fill our hearts with joy and hope as we await the return of Jesus Christ in glory. May we always be prepared to welcome Christ, and to share with others our faith in the life to come. We ask this through the same Christ our saviour, who lives and reigns with you and the Holy Spirit, one God for ever and ever. Amen.

CHRISTMAS: Gentle God, in the still of the night the Virgin Mary gave birth to Jesus, our Redeemer. The Messiah so long expected had come into the world. Let us so ponder this great mystery of your love that our hearts may be filled with wonder and praise. We ask you this through the same Jesus our saviour, in the power of the Holy Spirit. Amen.

LENT: Just and merciful God, in the preaching of John the Baptist you call us to repent of our sins and live according to your will. As we prepare to celebrate the Easter Mysteries, let us imitate Mary the mother of Jesus in her virtue, her courage and her faith. We ask this through Jesus Christ who lives and reigns with you and the Holy Spirit, one God for ever and ever. Amen.

EASTER: God of glory, Jesus Christ suffered and died out of love for us, and was raised from the dead on the third day as the scriptures had foretold. Like Mary the mother of Jesus, we share in his suffering. May we, like her, share also in his glory. We make this prayer to you through the same Jesus Christ, in the love of the Holy Spirit. Amen.

PENTECOST: God of power and might, you sent your Holy Spirit to the Apostles and to Mary the mother of Jesus, gathered with them in prayer. Fill us with that same Spirit, that we too may bear witness to your greatness and power. We ask this through Christ our Lord. Amen.

(Other suitable prayers may be found in the Breviary.)

PRAYING AT HOME

The following pages are to help you pray at home so that your prayer with Our Lady to God may continue to grow. The ways of praying described here are suggestions and can go with your usual ways of prayer.

PRAYING TO GOD LIKE WE TALK TO EACH OTHER
Prayer can be like WRITING A LETTER.
Find a quiet place, at home or in church; set aside some time — perhaps twenty minutes or so. Imagine you are writing a letter to God. Tell him what you've been doing, how you've been feeling. Tell him things that have made you happy, things that have made you sad. Thank him for all the good things he has given you, for health, for life, for family, for friends. Ask him for all your needs, for yourself and for others; ask him to help you grow in faith, in hope and in love. The reply might not come straight away, but it will come.

Prayer can be like MAKING A TELEPHONE CALL.
Whenever you have a couple of minutes, have a conversation with God. Speak to him in your heart, and give him time to speak to you. Tell him what's on your mind, what you need, for yourself and for others. If you are interrupted, come back to the conversation whenever you can — God does not lose patience.

Prayer can be like WRITING A POSTCARD.
Quite often we don't seem to have much time for praying, and we can't find the peace and quiet that we need. At times like this, we make short prayers, to keep God in our minds, to share our lives with him. We pray: 'Sorry Lord, I haven't much time', 'Wish you were here', 'Please God, give me your help' and any prayer like this. This might be the kind of prayer we make most often, but it is important that we don't forget other types of prayer.

PRAYING THE SCRIPTURES
Set aside a few minutes when you can sit quietly without being disturbed.

After a couple of minutes silence in the presence of God, open the New Testament of the bible and turn to one of the passages suggested below. Read the passage slowly, two or three times, and close your eyes, thinking about it, and reflecting on how it is relevant to your life.

Ask yourself what is God trying to say to you here. Is he encouraging you in your faith? Is he challenging you to be stronger in your faith? Is he showing you how you should relate to others? Is he telling you once again of his mercy and his power?

Use the thoughts that this part of scripture suggests to you in prayer to God. Tell him how you feel; ask him for what you need, for yourself and for others; thank him for all his gifts to you.

End by saying, in silence, 'Glory be to the Father, and to the Son, and to the Holy Spirit, as it was in the beginning, is now, and ever shall be, world without end; Amen.
Mother of Perpetual Help, Pray for me.'

SUGGESTED PASSAGES OF SCRIPTURE
When you want to thank God.
Psalm (115) — see page 7.
Luke 17:11-19.
1 Thessalonians 5:16-18.

When you want to ask God for something.
Luke 11:1-13.
John 14:12-14.
Romans 8: 26-28.

When you want to praise God.
Psalm 113 — see page 18.
Luke 1:46-55 The Magnificat; see page 10, & p.24 onwards.
Romans 8:31-39.

The above are just examples — the riches of scripture are endless.

(To look up a reference, for example Luke 1:46-55, find Luke in the contents of your bible. 1 is the chapter number, 46-55 are the relevant verses. Where there is a number before the name of the book, it means there is more than one work in the bible by the same author, and you are shown which work is the relevant one. For example, 1 Thessalonians 5:16-18 refers to St. Paul's first letter to the Thessalonians, chapter five, verses sixteen to eighteen).

TRADITIONAL PRAYERS

The Memorare

Remember,
O most gracious virgin Mary,
that never was it known,
that anyone fled to your protection,
implored your help,
or sought your intercession,
and was left unaided.
Inspired with this confidence,
we fly unto you,
O Virgin of virgins our Mother.
To you do we come,
before you we stand
sinful and sorrowful.
O Mother of the Word Incarnate,
despise not our petitions,
but in your mercy,
hear and answer us.

Hail, Holy Queen

Hail! Holy Queen,
Mother of mercy,
Hail! our life, our sweetness and our hope.
To thee do we cry,
poor banished children of Eve.
To thee do we send up our sighs,
mourning and weeping in this vale of tears.
Turn then, most gracious advocate,
thine eyes of mercy towards us.
And after this our exile,
show unto us the blessed fruit of thy womb, Jesus.
O Clement, O loving, O sweet Virgin Mary.

Hail Mary

Hail, Mary, full of grace.
The Lord is with thee.
Blessed art thou amongst women
and blessed is the fruit of thy womb, Jesus.
Holy Mary, mother of God,
pray for us sinners now
and at the hour of our death. Amen.

The Angelus

The Angel of the Lord declared to Mary:
And she conceived by the Holy Spirit.
Hail Mary...

Behold the handmaid of the Lord:
Be it done to me according to your word.
Hail Mary...

And the Word was made flesh:
And dwelt among us.
Hail Mary...

Pray for us, O holy Mother of God.
That we may be made worthy of the promises of Christ.

Let us pray.
Pour forth we beseech you, O Lord, your grace into our hearts
that we, to whom the incarnation of Christ, your Son, was
made known by the message of an angel, may be brought by
his passion and cross to the glory of his resurrection, through
the same Christ our Lord. Amen.

Published by
Redemptorist Publications

Text: Ed Hone, C.Ss.R.
Design: Roger Smith

Copyright © 1991 Redemptorist Publications
A Registered Charity limited by guarantee
Registered in England 3261721

First Printing .... April 1991
Seventh Printing .... March 2002 (35th thousand)

ISBN 0 85231 130 3

Printed in Britain by Polar Print Leicester LE4 9TZ

The Publishers are grateful to the following for use of copyright material:

S Anne Carter RSCJ for 'My soul proclaims the Lord my God' © 1988 by Religious of the
Sacred Heart. Timothy Dudley Smith, for 'Tell out, my soul' from 'Lift Every Heart', Collins
Liturgical Publications 1984. Mr Michael Hodgetts for the translation of 'God fills me with
joy', by Jean-Paul Lécot. Kevin Mayhew Ltd. for 'As I kneel before you' by Maria Parkinson
and 'Holy Virgin by God's decree' by Jean-Paul Lécot, translated by Rt. Rev. Mgr. W.R.
Lawrence; copyright Kevin Mayhew Ltd. Reproduced by permission from Hymns Old &
New, Licence No. 192052. A.P. Watt Ltd. on behalf of The Grail, England, for Psalms 24, 42,
46, 113, 115, 116, & 130, from 'The Grail Psalms: an Inclusive Language Version' published
by Wm Collins Sons & Co. Ltd., and The Magnificat 'My soul glorifies the Lord.'

Redemptorist

P U B L I C A T I O N S

Alphonsus House Chawton Hampshire GU34 3HQ
Telephone 01420 88222   Fax 01420 88805
rp@ShineOnline.net   www.ShineOnline.net